AF583755

PLATYPUS BEND

Diane Jackson Hill Craig Smith

The rivulet begins high on a mountain top. The water plummets over boulders and stumbles through crevices until it reaches a valley in a faraway place.

Its freshness sparkles as it gushes and splutters over pebbles and rocks. It twists and turns and turns and twists, until it swirls around a bend and softens into a calm pool …

No-one knows, but in that pool there is a secret.

The water makes a long ripple
as strong flippers power her along.

Bubbles pop as she dives deep and the
air is squeezed from her thick fur.

Circles radiate as she catches and crunches larvae, shellfish and worms with her soft, leathery bill.

A mate visits, but no-one notices when there are sometimes two of them, playing chasey round-and-round in the last of the day's shadows.

Mysterious clouds of mud ooze into the water as she tucks in her webbed feet and uses her claws to dig a long burrow into the bank.

She knows of the risks that threaten. She must choose the safest place. Sometimes the river floods, but her nest must stay dry.

She knows of the dangers that lurk. She seals the entrance with mud each time she crawls in or out, keeping her hide-out undetectable.

She cosies the nest with wet leaves,
spindly twigs and soft grasses.

Hidden at the end of her burrow, no-one could guess that she has now laid two precious eggs.

She carefully wraps her body around them to keep them snug, and then she waits.

She doesn't need to wait too long. Two tiny and pink clear-skinned babies tear open their shells and tumble out onto their mother's soft belly.

They suckle warm milk from patches on her skin.

Each day, at dawn or dusk, she sneaks out of the burrow to feed.

Tucked away in the nest, the babies' eyes are opening. Fine, velvety hair is covering their skin.

The time has come. Watchful and wary, she unplugs the burrow and the nestlings venture into the water.

She must teach them how to swim, to fossick for food and to protect themselves.

Platypus were always in this place,
but only some knew …

Platypus Particulars

- The platypus (scientific name *Ornithorhynchus anatinus*) is native to Australia. They live in freshwater habitats in the eastern and south-eastern parts of the country. Platypus can be found in Tasmania, Victoria, New South Wales, Canberra and Queensland.
- Platypus are 'monotremes', which are mammals that lay eggs. The only other animals classed as monotremes are the echidnas, of which there are four species.
- Platypus breathe air but spend most of their time fossicking for food underwater. They hunt with their eyes closed, using their sensitive bills to pick up the movement of prey in the water.

- Male platypus have poisonous spurs on their back legs, which can be used to defend their territory.
- Platypus float on the surface of the water to eat, grinding their food using coarse plates inside their bills.
- The thick, soft fur of platypus is resistant to water, which helps them stay warm while swimming. Their fur is also biofluorescent, which means that under certain ultraviolet (UV) light platypus fur glows in shades of green or purple.
- Female platypus lay a small number of eggs, which hatch in about ten days.
- Young platypus leave the nest when they are about four months old and almost fully grown. Platypus are quite solitary animals, often living in their own section of a waterway.
- Platypus are most active at twilight and through the night, but can be seen during the day.

Taking Care of Platypus Habitat

Communities find that when they clean up their local waterway, aquatic insects and other invertebrates return. These small creatures provide a plentiful food source for platypus. Vegetation can be planted along the edges of waterways to stabilise the bank, so platypus burrows can be strongly braced by the earth around them. This kind of planting also helps stop loose soil from muddying the water.

The Great Australian Platypus Search is a citizen scientist project that began in Victoria, Australia. Its aim is to reverse the 'Near Threatened Species' status of the platypus. As platypus are elusive and often difficult to spot, this project uses water samples to detect signs of platypus living in rivers and waterways.

Thanks to Louey for taking me in search of platypus. DJH

For Hemi. And for the Healesville Sanctuary, where little Hemi and I watched the platypus swim. CS

Previously a primary school teacher, **Diane Jackson Hill** is an award-winning children's author. She lives along the southern coast of Australia and is strongly drawn to the beauty of its plants and animals.

Diane is passionate about connecting children to the beauty of our incredible world and encouraging their awareness of its fragility.

Platypus Bend is the fourth title in Diane and Craig's environmental book partnership—three of them in collaboration with Museums Victoria.

Previous titles include *Chooks in Dinner Suits*, *Windcatcher* and *Saving Seal: the plastic predicament.* All three have received CBCA Notable awards, with *Chooks in Dinner Suits* also winning the Wilderness Society's Environment Award for Children's Literature in Picture Fiction in 2017, *Saving Seal* shortlisted for the same award in 2022, and *Windcatcher* winning a Whitley Award in 2020.

@dianejacksonhillkidsauthor

Craig Smith was raised in country South Australia, later training at the South Australian School of Art in Adelaide. In a forty year career he has illustrated many beloved and award-winning books for children.

Craig spends a great deal of time out in nature, whether he's tending his garden or venturing further afield to camp, bushwalk or ride his bike.

One compelling theme in front of Australians now is the need to pay attention to the environment. To learn more about it. To try and understand. To take responsibility for a patch of it. To be in it, enjoy it, and share it.

craigsmithillustration.com

First published in 2025 by
Museums Victoria Publishing
11 Nicholson Street
Carlton, Victoria 3053, Australia
publications@museum.vic.gov.au
www.museumsvictoria.com.au

A catalogue record for this book is available from the National Library of Australia

ISBN 9781921833762

Design by Julia Donkersley
Production by Sasha Beekman

Printed in China by RR Donnelley Asia Printing Solutions, Ltd.

1 3 5 7 9 10 8 6 4 2

Museums Victoria acknowledges the Wurundjeri Woi Wurrung and Boon Wurrung Bunurong peoples of the eastern Kulin Nations where we work, and First Peoples across Victoria and Australia. Our organisation, in partnership with the First Peoples of Victoria, is working to place First Peoples living cultures and histories at the core of our practice.

This book has been created by Museums Victoria, Australia's largest public museum organisation. Our venues include Melbourne Museum, Scienceworks, Immigration Museum and Royal Exhibition Building. Proceeds from the sale of this book support Museums Victoria's collections and ongoing research.